W9-CNQ-130

GHOSTS OF GALENA

Compiled by
Daryl Watson

Cover Photograph by
Daryl Watson

All Photographs
property of Galena/Jo Daviess County
Historical Society

Printed by
Gear House, Inc.
Galena, Illinois

Reprinted in 2004 by Welu Printing Company
Dubuque, Iowa

Copyright 1995
Galena/Jo Daviess County Historical Society

PREFACE

Ghosts of Galena is about real homes and real people. The individuals who have given us stories have done so voluntarily, happy to share a tale or two. Many still live or work in these same places. They have enjoyed their experiences and are willing to share them--up to a point. They still value their privacy and do not wish to have it invaded. As a result, we have disguised the identity of homes and individuals except where noted.

We hope you understand. Galena attracts well over 1,000,000 visitors annually, and even a small fraction wandering around a private home would make life unbearable. We ask, therefore, that everyone respect the private property and privacy of those involved.

ACKNOWLEDGEMENTS

Many individuals have helped make this book possible. They come from all walks of life and engage in all kinds of occupations. They share, however, a common bond with Galena's history and heritage. It is their desire that *Ghosts of Galena* add to the folklore and fascination that is so much a part of this historic community.

While there are too many to name individually, we must, however, single out Brodbeck Enterprises, parent corporation of Dick's Supermarkets, which provided a generous grant to the Historical Society to cover the cost of printing this book. Without their support, this book would not have been possible.

*U.S. Grant overlooking the historic community
of Galena, Illinois.*

INTRODUCTION

Ghosts! Are there really ghosts? Do they really haunt houses? And are any of those haunted homes in Galena?

We at the Historical Society don't know for certain, but over the years we have collected quite a number of stories from many different sources. Certainly the idea of ghosts and hauntings is nothing new. We found a number of tales in old Galena newspapers, the first in 1845.

In point of fact, fear of the unknown and explanations for the unexplained are as old as humankind. In the past we talked of superstitions, witchcraft and old wives' tales. Today we talk of the supernatural and paranormal. Our search for answers continues because we are beings who need to know.

Ghosts are explained today (or explained away) by many different theories. A common one holds that there is a spirit world with good and bad spirits. The evil ones are ready to confuse and confound--or worse--to possess. The good ones are ready to guide and protect.

Many of us, however, believe ghosts to be disembodied spirits who, for whatever reason, have failed to move on. They are trapped, either through design or desire, in a netherworld bordering our own. We often believe that a traumatic death led to their plight and that some wrong must be made right before their spirit can move onward.

Others suggest that ghostly phenomena are extensions of ourselves; that swinging light, eerie feeling or thumping in the night may be something only we can experience. Perhaps we create the manifestations subconsciously.

Still others believe strange sights and sounds to be energy traces left by some dramatic event years ago. They are like ripples in a pond, becoming ever fainter as time advances. Individuals with acute sensory powers can pick them up; others cannot.

Modern science has taken a rather skeptical view of the spirit world, seeking to discount and discredit stories and beliefs. There is a logical explanation for everything, science suggests; we simply need to find it.

Logical or not, something out there is happening. Over the last 10-12 years we have talked to many residents of Galena (both old and new) about strange happenings in their homes. We were amazed at how many had a story to tell. Over 60 percent had experienced something unexplained. Our informal and unscientific surveys revealed that roughly one-third believed in a ghostly spirit, one-third were skeptics and one-third simply didn't know.

Most of our confidants are well-educated, well-travelled and well-read people. They are not into alternative lifestyles and UFO abductions. Many recounted their experiences very matter-of-factly, believing in retrospect that it could be explained. But whether explainable or not, the events added to the mystique of owning an older home. There is, after all, nothing more rewarding than a mystery in need of a solution.

Galena's ghosts are a relatively benign lot. No one has reported flying furniture, blood-stained walls or possession. It seems unfortunate that television and tabloids have emphasized this facet of hauntings. Our homeowners encountered non-threatening things--such as sights, sounds and smells that could not readily be explained. Sometimes it was just a "feeling" of another presence.

The overwhelming majority of hauntings occurred when new home-owners first moved into an older home or first began a major remodeling project. It was then that lights would come on, doors would close and mysterious footsteps would be heard. As time passed, so too, did the strange occurrences. As one homeowner put it: "The spirits got used to us, and we got used to them."

"Why should a historical society be interested in ghosts and strange phenomena?" you might ask. Quite simply, they are a part of our folklore and culture. Stories, true or not, are told to enlighten and amuse. They are passed from generation to generation and become a part of our lives and our community. They help define our thinking--who we are and how we feel about ourselves and our world. Whether the stories originated last week or last century makes no difference. They are still a part of us.

With that in mind, please take a few minutes to ponder the following tales. We hope you'll enjoy reading them as much as we have enjoyed collecting them. And if you have one to share, let us know!

TABLE OF CONTENTS

How It All Started. 3

Ghosts. 11

The Hanging of John Taylor 15

O'Leary's Experience with a Ghost 20

Too Good to Keep 22

She Knows It was a Real Ghost. 24

The Pale Horse 26

Common Sense and Reason 28

The Flower Pot Affair 29

No Graveyard Ghosts for Him. 30

Galena has a Ghost!!! 32

The Ghost of the Railroad Man--Revisited?. 34

The Ghost of Turner Hall 37

Turner Hall Revisited 39

Bradner Smith Visitations 41

The Indian Boy 45

Guest Presence 47

Refreshing Spirits 50

Don't Blame the Dog 53

Breaking Glass and Gusts of Air 56

O.C. Welch and Family. 58

A Guest House with Uninvited Guests 64

Nuns and Voices 67

Bagpipes a Playing. 69

Leslie. 71

The Man in the Brown Suit. 77

Footsteps in the Night 79

The Husband Who Wouldn't Leave. 81

Margaret 84

Children at Play 87

Paula 91

The museum—where it all started.

HOW IT ALL STARTED

We at the Galena History Museum have always been interested in ghosts. We had heard stories over the years about this place or that place. Galena was the perfect place for such things, too. It had lots of history and lots of old homes. Given the age of houses and the many families that have inhabited them, how could there not be stories? We might never have gone beyond the wondering stage, however, had it not been for a series of personal experiences in our own museum, located at 211 S. Bench St.

This mansion turned museum was constructed by Daniel Barrows in 1858 shortly after a fire had levelled his previous home on the same site. Barrows was a mover and shaker in Galena. He owned a distillery, a confectionery store and later, a lumber yard. When hard times came after the Civil War, he lost heavily (as did many who stayed in Galena). His wife died and later the creditors came. He had to give up his mansion.

The home remained as a residence until 1922 when the Odd Fellows Lodge purchased it. They removed a rear wing of the house and built a large two-story hall in its place. It served their purposes and that of the community until the depression came. Forced to sell, they gave up the property to the City of Galena in 1938. City Hall moved into the front two rooms of the first floor. A newly created museum association took over the remaining space through a 99 year lease agreement. The City moved out in 1967 leaving the entire property for use by the historical society.

Our first inkling that something was going on came in the spring of 1989. It was then that we heard strange footsteps. Almost as a joke, we decided to start a file in the computer. Every time something happened, we'd enter an account of the activity. Following, then, are the entries made by two of us:

January, 1989 (Doug)--It was a quiet morning during the off season and Gayle and I were at our respective desks in the second floor office. No one else was in the building, or so we thought . . . Suddenly, we both heard what sounded like a bumping or shuffling noise going down the steps. I thought it sounded like someone quickly shuffling down the stairway. The sound continued for two to three seconds, so it was not the building creaking or settling with the colder weather.

"Did you hear that?" I immediately asked Gayle.

"Yes."

"Is there anyone in the building?"

"I don't think so."

With this, I immediately opened my office door, jumped out into the hallway and looked down the stairway.

The sound of footsteps moved along the hallway.

Nothing. Then began a 20 minute search in which both Gayle and I scoured the building top to bottom to ascertain a likely explanation for the sound. None was found--even though we checked for birds, rodents, falling plaster in the walls, a settling building--or even a practical joke! There was, quite simply, no logical explanation.

(It was at this time that Gayle entered an experience of hers that had happened the year before.)

April, 1988 (Gayle)--Following the opening reception of our new Pioneer Exhibit, I was closing up the museum and walked through the door into the large hall where it was now pitch black. As I slowly walked toward the steps, I passed an old upright piano. Just as I walked past, a chord played on the piano. Having no desire to investigate, I raced out of the building and on home. (I did, of course, remember to lock up and set the alarm system!)

January 9, 1990 (Doug)--I had returned briefly to the museum after closing to retrieve some papers in my second floor office. Upon leaving the office and starting down the stairs, I distinctly heard a thumping sort of noise begin at the top of the stairs and descend with me. The sound was almost like someone shuffling down the steps. It seemed to have started in the wall at the top of the steps, but descended with me--it was almost like it passed through me--and then moved laterally out into the hallway!

I stopped two-thirds of the way down the steps and looked back along the lower hallway. The light was dim, but absolutely no one, or no thing, was visible. Upon reaching the foot of the steps, a second, and more sinister sound was heard . . . that of a hard-soled shoe sliding across the tile floor. This sound was very distinctive and came from the area of the drinking fountain underneath the stairway. I heard it not once, but several times in succession. Each time it was as if someone were sweeping, or dragging their sole across that section of floor. I reached over and turned the hall lights on and then swiftly walked back to the drinking fountain area.

I was sure someone was playing a trick on me. But there was no one . . . nothing at all. All was quiet.

March 28, 1990 (Gayle)--I was closing up the museum and was about to lock the door when I heard shuffling footsteps in the hall. The sounds were unmistakable, yet no one else was in the building!

April 6, 1990 (Gayle)--I was in the building taking care of a couple of things after hours. Not wanting to be spooked, I had brought my husband and son along. I was in the washroom area with my son when I heard what sounded like a piece of furniture being moved upstairs in the large hall. My husband was up there and I thought it was him. When I went upstairs, however, and asked him if he had moved something, he said "no". He hadn't touched a thing.

July 16, 1990 (Gayle)--Doug and I were talking in my office when suddenly I noticed the chandelier in the adjacent office swaying to and fro. It was the first time that either of us had ever noticed it moving. Doug thought it was the fan from the air-conditioner, but the chandelier continued to sway intermittently, ever so slightly, even after the unit was turned off.

September 10, 1990 (Doug)--It was 6:08 P.M. and I was the only one in the building, waiting for the monthly board meeting to begin at 7:00 P.M. While fiddling with the radio to catch some news, I became aware of sounds downstairs. It sounded like someone was down there, walking around in the hallway. With the radio turned off, I listened intently. I could also make out some light, indistinct tapping or knocking noises. And then the stairs creaked--just like someone was coming up to the office! But then it stopped and there was nothing more. Whoever, or whatever, was gone.

September 18, 1990 (Doug)--I was working late in the upstairs office when a squeak from a floorboard out in the hallway caught my attention. The only time those boards ever squeak is when someone walks on them. I then heard footsteps--or what sounded like them--move along the hallway until they were just outside the door to my office. I thought surely that someone was still in the building and was coming to the office.

I looked over at the doorknob, fully expecting it to turn and the door to open. But nothing happened. Growing impatient--or anxious--I grabbed the knob and opened the door fully expecting to greet someone . But I was wrong, for there was no one and all was quiet.

January, 1991 (Doug)--After Gayle left for a new job in November of 1990, the museum seemed to quiet down. In fact, the staff specifically noted the absence of ghostly happenings. There was some speculation that Gayle had taken the hapless ghost with her, but then came the night of our "mini-taste of Galena". It was the project of a local dining and lodging establishment and was to be a reception for VIPs holding a convention. Little did their servers know what was in store for them at the museum.

It started when one of the waitresses serving champagne to the arriving guests suddenly and unexplainably dropped her entire tray, sending the bubbly liquid all over the floor. Little attention was paid, however, and the mess was quickly cleaned up. But it wasn't more than 10 minutes later when a second server suddenly noticed the full glasses on her tray begin to tremble. Before she could steady things, the glasses and tray tumbled to the floor.

At this point, the person in charge admonished her servers to be much more careful. This was all the more embarrassing because these workers were all seasoned veterans of events such as this and had served drinks in this manner many times.

It was at this point that I (after having surveyed the damage) was standing in the gift shop when a tray with 8-10 champagne glasses--sitting alone on the gift shop counter--

Champagne glasses were tumbling to the floor.

caught my attention. This was the preparation counter where glasses and trays were made ready for the next serving. But with no one near, the plastic glasses began to shake. Before anyone could rush over to prevent loss, more than half toppled from the tray onto the counter. The servers were once again admonished in the sternest terms to be careful--there was yet one more group of VIPs to come. For this, three waitresses with full trays were lined up along the hallway awaiting their arrival. I was the fourth in line, waiting to present a slide show.

Suddenly, without a bit of warning, the glasses on the tray being held by the girl next to me began to shake. She quickly took hold of the tray with both hands, but the glasses began to topple, despite the tray by this time being held rock steady. Under her breath, I heard her say: "Oh, sh--! I don't believe this!" Once again, over half of a tray's drinks ended up on the floor. Since I was standing immediately next to her I was able to see and hear everything. "How could this have happened again?" I wondered. We were all incredulous.

Afterwards, when we were putting everything away, the co-ordinator in charge told me that she had never before had so many embarrassing mishaps. Some blamed it on the plastic champagne glasses which were light and spindly, but others of us wondered. We joked that it was the ghost of first resident Daniel Barrows, who as the owner of a distillery, no doubt preferred spirits of another kind.

December, 1991 (Doug)--Once again, some of us were musing about the absence of our ghost, last experienced during the champagne episode. Imagine our surprise, however, when our part time employee for the summer, Donna, told us that she had heard our "friend" on more than one occasion.

It's presence had taken the form of footsteps and knocking on the wall. The last time, not more that a week ago, occurred as she was closing up and was counting the money at the gift shop counter. She was surprised to hear footsteps that seemed to be upstairs, like someone coming down from the big exhibit hall. They seemed to continue along the upstairs hallway, terminating with a sliding shoe sound, as if someone were sliding the sole of their shoe across a gritty floor.

That was the second time that Donna had heard this distinctive sound. Having worked at the museum all summer, Donna was very familiar with the normal sounds associated with the building, including the pigeons. She had never heard our previous ghost stories, however, and volunteered her experiences only after we joked about our mysterious footsteps. For us the mystery remains.

We've heard nothing more from our museum "ghost" since 1991. We did, however, discover that he's been around a while. Staff at the museum years ago recalled gift shop merchandise being tampered with. They said he especially liked their licorice. And there was the woman visitor who asked who the strangely dressed man in the slide room was. When asked minutes later to point him out, he was gone, yet no one had left the building.

But the real treat came when we were told of a City Council meeting being conducted by Mayor Logan over forty years ago when the building was still City Hall. Only a few were attending when suddenly a terrible commotion was heard in the upstairs hallway. With no one else in the building they all looked at each other and then rushed up the stairs to see what mischief was afoot. Just like our experience years later, they were greeted with silence. Everything was in order. There was no one to be found.

(Given our experiences at the museum, we determined to search through early Galena newspapers to see if there were any ghostly tales from days gone by. Indeed there were! Following, then, are a number of those stories, reprinted exactly as they first appeared:)

"A regular ghost scene came off here last week."

"GHOSTS"

(From the January 17, 1845
Weekly Northwestern Gazette)

"It may not be amiss to give greater publicity to the fact that a regular ghost scene came off here last week in the lower part of the city in a small tenement of one room which was occupied by a couple of females. There they lived in virtuous retirement, enjoying two of the greatest luxuries of a cold winter's night in a northern climate, a bed and a stove, and time passed on with them just as rapidly as with all the rest of the world. One night, after carefully pulling the latch-string of the door, and looking under the bed, of course, to make sure that no intruder lay there in ambush, they laid down--but not to sleep! Right opposite to them, standing against the wall, there appeared a tall man in the attitude of continually beckoning to them with his long arms, as though he wished them to follow him. They knew it to be a ghost, though contrary to all history of tradition of spectral etiquette, the obtruding gentleman had a broad red face on . . . It was unaccountable. It is an innovation that requires to be looked into by the Temperance Society, and its cause ferreted out. It was conjectured that the specter's anxiety to induce the females to follow him arose from a duty to unfold to them some tale of murder, perhaps to point them to the secret place of deposit of the bones of its once corporeal frame, that the guilty might be brought to justice . . . Be that as it may, the women in the bed refused to obey the palavering signs of the aforesaid gentleman with a red face, but strenuously clung to each other in the very spirit of the proverb, that 'misery loves company'. Whereupon, they do positively assert, that he became wroth, and did many unseemly things which no honest well-mannered ghost would do, such as knocking over the candlestick, shaking the bedstead even till it fell down, and scattering coals of fire about the room! This was rough usage from such a customer, and they soon abandoned the house to the sole occupancy of the unwelcome tenant.

The particulars of the affair were soon known in the neighborhood. Then was the supposed history of that house first sifted out and written with the pen of marvel, and 'great the wonder grew' that divers mysterious occurrences had not undergone a judicial investigation 'at the time they happened'. However, to hasten along with our story, we skip over these sage surmises, which most people will listen to if they relate to the unfortunate poor, especially if a ghost is in the play, and say that a number of resolute fellows determined to have an interview with the uncivil apparition, at whatever hazard. We do not know that one went armed with a Bible in one coat pocket while the other was filled with rocks or which one it was that whistled psalm tunes the loudest during the considerable time they were kept in waiting. They had been told that it was not customary for the visitor to show himself, in fact it was an invariable rule with him not to enter until the candle was blown out, and after a while the light was extinguished--and sure enough, there the ghost was against the wall, with his red face on, and his long bony arms beckoning and clawing towards them with great energy and in a supplicating posture. One of the company had been a soldier in the last war. He refused to be made a prisoner at the surrender of Hull, on which occasion he leaped the pickets when he saw the treachery of the commander, and escaped. With equal valor he now stood his ground firmly. A council of war was called, and it was concluded by the flickering blaze shining through certain cracks in the side of the stove next to the wall, which required but little effort of an excited imagination to fashion into the appearance of a phantom of fright, sufficient to shake the wits well nigh out of two superstitious women and the bedstead.

But it is not the low and ignorant alone that allow the thought of such things to trouble them. There are few persons who like to go alone into what is called a 'haunted house' after nightfall. Much of this feeling is doubtless owing to a wrong education of children. Every heart has its fund of romance about these things. It is our privilege to derive pleasure as well as pain from their contemplation. Such is the law implanted in the mind. Sir Walter Scott remarks of some of the old superstitions of the North of England: 'We almost envy the credulity of those who, in the gentle moonlight of a summer night, amid the tangled glades of a deep forest, or on the turfy swell of her romantic commons, could fancy they saw the fairies tracing their sportive ring. But it is in vain to regret illusions which, however engaging, must of necessity yield their place before the increase of knowledge, like the shadows at the advance of morn.' We like the views of celebrated Addison on the subject of ghosts and supernatural apparitions. He says,--'were I a father, I should take a particular care to preserve my children from these little horrors of imagination which they are apt to contract when they are young and are not able to shake off when they are in years. I have known a soldier that has entered a breach affrighted at his own shadow and look pale upon a little scratching at his door, who the day before had marched up against a battery of cannon. There are instances of persons who have been terrified, even to distraction, at the figure of a tree or the shaking of a bulrush. The truth of it is, I look upon a sound imagination as the greatest blessing of life, next to a clear judgement and a good conscience. In the meantime, since there are very few whose minds are not more or less subject to these dreadful thoughts and apprehensions, we ought to arm ourselves against them by the dictates of reason and religion, to pull the old woman out of our hearts (as Perseus expresses it) and extinguish those impertinent notions which we imbibed at a time that we were not able to judge of their absurdity. Or, if we believe, as many wise and good men have done, that there are such phantoms and apparitions as those I have been speaking of, let us endeavor to establish to ourselves an interest in Him who holds the reins of the whole creation in His hand, and moderates them after such a manner, that it is impossible for one being to break loose upon another without his knowledge and permission. For my own part, I am apt to join in opinion with those who believe that all the regions of nature swarm with spirits and that we have multitudes of spectators on all our actions, when we think ourselves most alone; but, instead of terrifying myself with such a notion, I am wonderfully pleased to think that I am always engaged with such innumerable society, in searching out the wonders of creation, and joining in the same concert of praise and adoration'."

"THE HANGING OF JOHN TAYLOR"

(Jo Daviess County's first–and only–legal hanging took place in 1855. Not surprisingly, it generated a tremendous amount of attention. Even today, it is still talked about with some saying that nothing will grow on the spot where they hung an innocent man. Following are several accounts describing the affair, the first from the 1878 Jo Daviess County History:)

"The first notable crime which was committed within the borders of the county was the murder of Mrs. Taylor by her husband, John I. Taylor, who suffered the death penalty as an atonement for the deed. Since that time, murderers have got off with various terms of imprisonment, from three years to life sentences. The facts connected with the Taylor murder were briefly as follows: Taylor resided in the upper story of a dilapidated frame house in Old Town, near the bank of the creek. A man by the name of Rosenburg occupied the first floor, and is said to have been on too intimate terms with Taylor's wife. One night in the month of October, 1854, Taylor reeled home drunk, and began to abuse his wife. Rosenburg heard the disturbance overhead, and went up for the purpose of quelling it. Taylor, enraged at the sight of the man whom he imagined was criminally intimate with his wife, seized a gun and struck at Rosenburg, who had turned for the purpose of fleeing down stairs. At that instant Mrs. Taylor stepped between the two men, and received the blow on the side of her own head, crushing in the skull.

As already stated, Taylor was arrested, tried, found guilty, and sentenced to be hanged. The death sentence was rendered by Judge Ben R. Sheldon, before whom the case was tried, on Thursday, November 30, 1854, and Taylor was ordered to be hanged on 'Friday, the nineteenth day of January next (1855), between the hours of ten o'clock in the forenoon and four o'clock in the afternoon of that day.' The verdict of the law was carried out on the day above named by W.R. Rowley, sheriff. The scaffold was erected on the poorhouse farm, and the execution was open, and witnessed by as many as five thousand people. That was the first and last execution in Jo Daviess County. It has been said that one of the principal witnesses, and the only important one against Taylor, confessed on his death-bed that he was the one who killed Mrs. Taylor, and that Taylor was innocent. As to the truth or untruth of this rumor the people differ. But, true or false, the confession, if one was made, came too late to save Taylor's life, or to affect him for either weal or woe."

He was sentenced to be hanged at the Jo Daviess County Courthouse.

"WHEN WAS TAYLOR HANGED?"

(From the March 13, 1884 Daily Gazette)

"Darlington, Wis., March 3.-Editor Gazette: A dispute has arisen here between two old settlers in regard to the date when Taylor was hanged for murdering his wife. One party claims that it was in 1854, and the other that it was before that year. Will you please settle the question and also give the name of the sheriff who did the job:

Respectfully,   OLD SETTLER

ANSWER

Taylor was hanged on the 19th day of January, 1855, by Sheriff W. R. Rowley, now County Judge of this county.

Taylor suspected an intimacy between his wife and an Italian who lived near by. Going home one evening, he found the Italian in company with his wife, and a quarrel ensued. In the course of the quarrel, Taylor hit his wife with his gun, and killed her. Taylor, in defense, set up the plea that in aiming a blow at the Italian, he hit his wife by accident; and to this day, many people here believe his statement was true. Taylor was the only person that was ever hanged in this county.

Sheriff Rowley prepared a gallows in the Court House yard; but as the day of the execution approached, many of that class of people who are afraid of ghosts, signed a petition requesting the sheriff to hang Taylor somewhere out of the city limits. He acceded to the request, and the hanging took place on the County Farm in East Galena, about two miles from the city."

"TRAGEDY OF THE HILLS"

(As excerpted from Rhythm of the River or Songs of Old Galena by Thomas J. McCarthy, Freeport: Freeport Printing Co., 1942.)

This little tale of river days,
Gleaned from historic past,
Is not a pleasant narrative,
So I've placed it toward the last.
Bare facts was all I ever learned,
Or old timers would recall,

They dismiss the memory from their mind,
'Twas the same with one and all.
The records in the Court House show,
They'd tell me--every one--
How a man was hung on Porter's Mound
For a crime he hadn't done.
'Twas on the banks of Meekers shallow creek,
In a stone house on the slope,
With his wife lived Mr. Taylor,
The victim of the rope.
The story goes that Taylor once,
As you and I might do,
Took on an extra load of grog
And started for the "Slough."
Then he met up with a stranger,
And they drank till tongues were thick,
'Twas thus they reached the Taylor home,
On the banks of Meeker Creek.
Yes, it is the same old story,
It often happens now,
Two merry drunks had lost their wits
And soon commenced to row.
An argument was started,
Came a battle then and there,
Unsteady fists were swinging,
Mostly hitting empty air.
The frightened wife rebuked them,
As around the room they milled;
She tried at last to part them,
But in doing so was killed.
She was struck down with a poker,
A mean weapon of defense,
It was grabbed up by the brawlers,
When the battle did commence.
They were brought back to their senses,
These men in drunken strife;
Next morn each blamed the other

For the death of Taylor's wife.
The case was brought before the court
With the stranger on the stand;
He swore that Mrs. Taylor's death
Was caused by Taylor's hand.
Heartbroken and remorseful,
So all the records state,
Taylor took the blame that day
For the murder of his mate.
Throughout the crowded courtroom
The judge's sentence rang--
"This prisoner here, called Taylor,
Pleads guilty--and must hang."
A scaffold made of heavy oak,
At the base of Porter's Mound,
Was erected by the sheriff
Upon the Poorhouse ground.
The crowd was large upon that day,
Just a morbid-loving gang,
They were led by curiosity,
To see a felon hang.
The noose was placed around his neck,
And with hood, he couldn't see,
Then the trap was sprung,
        And Taylor swung--into eternity.
Then all seemed still and lonesome,
Here and there was heard a sob,
Horseshoe Mound stood solemn witness,
As did her sister, Pilot Knob.
The crowd dispersed in silence,
All depressed with what they saw,
'Twas the first and only hanging,
By the town's official law.
Years after in Saint Louis,
A confession there was made
By a man who really did the deed
For which poor Taylor paid.

He plainly saw the figure of a woman, dressed in ghostly white.

"O'LEARY'S EXPERIENCE WITH A GHOST"

(*From the August 13, 1875 Galena Daily Gazette*)

"A female apparition has been cutting up capers of late, in the vicinity of Marshal O'Leary's house. The other evening that official repaired to the barn for the purpose of taking care of his horse, and while in the act of entering the stable door, he plainly saw by the light of the moon, the figure of a woman, dressed in a suit of ghostly white, and gazing full at him from out a pair of flaming eyes. Just at that instant the Marshal bethought himself of urgent business that required his immediate attention, and dropping his pail of water, he quickly made tracks for the house. Placing himself in front of a window, he watched for future developments, and in the course of time distinctly saw the apparition emerge from the barn and walk across the lot toward the wood-house. In view of the fact that it was only a woman (who couldn't vote, dead or alive) the Marshal mustered up courage, and buckling on his insignia of office, he stepped out of the door and cautiously approached the wan figure, which immediately vanished into thin air and was seen no more that night. The above facts are obtained from a perfectly reliable gentleman to whom the intrepid Tom told the story in his usual concise and comprehensive manner. Mrs. O'Leary asserts that the Marshal saw no ghosts that night, except those conjured up by spirits within, but the latter is willing to take his oath that it was a genuine representative from the other world and no mistake."

He drew a bead and let a streak of moonlight through the body!

"TOO GOOD TO KEEP"

(From the August 13, 1875 Daily Gazette)

"The other evening, a certain gentleman residing on Bench Street was engaged in disrobing for the night when he was suddenly startled by seeing the face of a man pressed against the window pane and peering boldly into his sleeping room. Naturally enough our friend bethought himself of burglars, and cried out 'who's there!' The supposed thief made no reply, but kept right on looking with all the eyes he had in his head. About this time the gentleman's dander began to raise, and donning his pantaloons and grasping a seven-shooter, he cautiously slipped out the front door and proceeding to the corner of the house, drew a bead upon the intruder and let a streak of moonlight through his body half an inch in diameter. He then went into the house and with "I've killed him", sank into a chair, while a deadly pallor overspread his countenance. At this juncture the ladies of the house rushed into the room with handkerchiefs stuffed in their mouths and their sides fairly bursting with laughter, dragging after them an effigy of a man made over a broom stick, which they had that evening prepared, and at a convenient season, stood up in front of the window. The joke was highly relished by the gentleman who laughed as loud as any one when fully convinced that his hands were not dyed with human blood, and demonstrated the fact that it would not be a healthful undertaking for burglars or anybody else to look into the windows of this particular Bench Street man, at unseasonable hours."

Some things are not what they seem.

"SHE KNOWS IT WAS A REAL GHOST"

(From the June 26, 1875 Daily Gazette)

"A comical incident occurred at the new Cemetery in this city not long ago, which is entirely too good to keep, although by some of our more punctilious readers, the story may be regarded as a little out of place in a public newspaper. However, the facts are as follows: A certain Galena lady repaired to the burying ground above mentioned the other evening, for the purpose of decorating the grave of her defunct husband with flowers. Arriving at the family lot in due time, the widow dropped upon her knees, and after offering a silent prayer, she began to arrange the plants upon the top of the mound under which rested in peace the bones of the late partner of her joys and sorrows. While in the act of reaching over for the purpose of inserting the roots of a vine in the earth, a pugnacious goat owned in that neighborhood and permitted to roam the grounds at will, with lowered head and elevated tail, sprang forward and striking the woman in weeds, fair and square from behind, knocked her heels over head and landed her almost fifteen feet on the opposite side of the grave. Of course the lady screamed, in fact yelled bloody murder, as almost anybody would under similar circumstances, and picking herself up, she ran from the premises at the top of her speed, and halting at the nearest house, fell half fainting into the door. When partly restored to consciousness, she informed the woman of the house that she had been attacked by a real genuine ghost, with flaming eyes and horned head, and to this very day it is an utter impossibility to convince the lady that it was anything else but the very evil one himself, or that it is conducive to health to sit in a hard-bottomed chair without a cushion. The above truthful facts have been furnished by a gentleman who, unobserved, was standing beside a grave in another part of the yard, when the comical drama was enacted."

*Suddenly they were aroused by a terrible clatter issuing
from the basement.*

"THE PALE HORSE"

(From the March 16, 1874 Daily Gazette)

"Galena has got the ghosts, in the most malignant form.
The first well-developed case made its appearance at the
residence of a gentleman on Bench Street, whose wife is
temporarily elsewhere on a visit to her relatives. On
Saturday last, our friend invited a courageous young man to
share his bed during the night, as sleeping with his wife's
nightdress had ceased to be a novelty. The "son of David"
consented, and after a perusal of the horrible experiences of a
traveling agent, as recounted in Saturday's Gazette, followed
by a lengthy conversation on ghosts in general, the two
retired to their sleeping room in the third story of the house,
having satisfactorily settled the question, in their own minds,
at least, that the ghost business was a fraud of the very worst
type. In the course of time, the two had ensconced
themselves upon the bed rail, and without speaking a word

to each other, were gradually falling into the arms of Morpheus, when they were aroused by a terrible clatter issuing, apparently, from the basement. The hair of these hitherto incredulous and courageous men began to elevate, until it stood on ends like quills upon a fretful porcupine. With trembling limbs and dismayed countenances, they emerged from under the bed clothes, and lighting a lamp, cautiously made their way down stairs, armed to the teeth with all the munitions of war the house afforded. Arriving at the basement, they discovered nothing, and were laughing over their momentary fright, when a like noise, though more terrific in its nature, was heard in the upper part of the house. If any of the readers of the Gazette have ever been in a like situation, they can sympathize with these two affrighted gentlemen, who were undecided as to whether it was best to call in the neighbors, bolt for the street, or lay right down and die in their tracks. A brief council of war was held, however, and our friends concluded to fight it out on that line, if it took until the morning. Our informant tells us that the balance of the night was spent by these two affrighted males in oscillating between the upper and lower part of the house, in search of the origin of the supernatural demonstrations, and that the mystery is yet unsolved."

"COMMON SENSE AND REASON"

(From the December 28, 1888 Galena Gazette)

"The nineteenth century is drawing to a close, and it is about time that superstition and the fears arising from it were giving place to a little common sense and reason. The old story about a ghost, or phantom miner, who is said to haunt mines near Galena, has been revived, and incredible and paradoxical as it may seem, yet it is a fact that the story is given credence by some people. There are mines near Pilot Knob in which it is said that men are almost afraid to work, alleging that they frequently hear strange, unnatural noises. But what is still more difficult to believe is that a farmer residing near one of these alleged haunted mines has sold his land and made preparations to vacate comfortable premises on account of fear arising from a belief in this ridiculous story. The story of haunted mines in the vicinity of Galena has been told so often, and the whiskers upon it have grown so long and gray, that it is with reluctance that we make this allusion to it. We simply state the facts, and request that the reader accept them for what they are worth."

A ghost, or phantom miner, is said to haunt mines near Galena.

Cracked pots disrupt neighborhood.

"THE FLOWER POT AFFAIR"

*(As quoted in a Dubuque Telegraph Herald article
dated October 29, 1982)*

"An 1897 Galena Gazette tells the story of one Mrs. John Armbruster (later to become a Mrs. Crouch), who lived on Spring Street, between High and Dodge streets in Galena.

Crouch was 'credited with the ability to take care of herself' and had reportedly threatened to return after death, if necessary, and 'give token of her displeasure' if things went awry.

The story goes that her prize possessions in life were her beautiful flowers and flower pots. Unfortunately, it seems that her husband didn't share this love, and following her death, he passed several of her pots on to a friend.

Before long the friend reported the pots were getting 'prankish,' jumping about and emitting strange noises. She tolerated this with some uneasiness for a few days, until, while she was sweeping, the largest of the pots was 'hurled by unseen hands' across the room to crash at her feet.

The terrified woman hastily broke up the remaining pots, and only then, says the story, did the color return to her cheeks."

He wouldn't go through any cemetery after dark.

"NO GRAVEYARD GHOSTS FOR HIM"

(From the March 27, 1909 Daily Gazette)

Galenian Walks Two Miles Around Rather Than Go Through Greenwood Cemetery In the Dark

"If you had been out hunting all day, and had bagged nary a duck, and you were so tired from wading in the mud that you could hardly drag one foot ahead of the other--which would you rather do, go home by a short cut that would necessitate your passing through a cemetery after dark, or go two miles around by another road? That was the proposition a well-known Galena business man, ex-alderman, member of a prominent lodge, baseball fan, enthusiastic hunter, etc., etc., was up against the other night, and inasmuch as he was so near petered out by the tramp that he could hardly walk and inasmuch as he preferred to add two more long weary miles to his journey, the inference is plain, (so his friends affirm, at least) that the only reason why he refused to take the short cut was because he was afraid to tackle that jaunt through the cemetery after dark. This well known G.B.M et.al., had been down the river with a friend for two days and a night and had got only one measly duck. At the close of the second day they decided to return home and with mud to their boot tops began the heart breaking journey. Now one of the hunters wanted to take the shortcut through Greenwood, which would save probably two miles of walking, but the Galena business man, not he, wouldn't go through any cemetery after dark no matter how much walking he could save, and to make a long story short--the bespattered and bedraggled party of two finally got home, but not until they were so fagged that they could hardly crawl. The longest way round may or may not be the shortest way home, but it is the safest way home--at least that is what one Galena man thinks, when it comes to going through cemeteries after dark."

"Every night, lantern in hand, he goes from the Mound to Shot Tower Hill . . ."

"GALENA HAS A GHOST!!!"

(From the November 7, 1907 Galena Weekly Gazette)

Specter is Seen Prowling Around Nightly With Lantern, Between Horseshoe Mound and School Section

"Do you believe in ghosts? Perhaps you laugh at this question and say there are no such things. Then possibly you do not live on School Section, and probably you have not seen the ghost that crosses the stretch of country every evening from Horseshoe Mound to Shot Tower Hill.

Ghosts have been reported on the Turnpike and other parts of the city in years past, and their midnight meanderings spread terror and fear to the hearts of those who saw them. During the last few nights a number of the residents of the School Section have confessed that they have seen a ghostly apparition which starts from the vicinity of Horseshoe Mound and takes its way slowly yet none the less certainly across the space between that place and Shot Tower

Hill. The apparition is reported to appear about seven-thirty or eight o'clock each evening, and has the resemblance of a man carrying a lantern.

Some of those who watch with fear, stilled hearts and bated breath, say that the apparition is the ghost of a railroad man who was killed as the result of a collision between two trains on the Illinois Central tracks near the stock yards a half dozen or more years ago. They say that his spirit cannot rest, and that every night, lantern in hand, he goes from the Mound to Shot Tower Hill and then vanishes as mysteriously as he appeared.

Be this as it may, not a few of the good people living on and near School Section are positive that they have seen the apparition. You do not believe in ghosts, you say. Well, perhaps the apparition will appear again this evening. Perhaps, too, you will see it with your own eyes, and if you do you will doubtless be convinced."

(Galena Has a Ghost!!! concludes our selection of early Galena Tales. You can see, as did we, that ghost stories are nothing new in Galena. They've been around since the founding of the town. But are they still with us? Following are some of the present-day tales which we have collected. As you will see, strange and unexplained happenings are still very much with us and still very much a part of us!)

It was not a distinct face . . . but it was definitely a human face.

"THE GHOST OF THE RAILROAD MAN--REVISITED?"

Could the ghost of the railroad man, as reported by the Gazette in 1907, still be with us today? We wondered, particularly when the following tale came to us from a motorist who experienced something while driving around Horseshoe Mound.

Everyone familiar with Galena knows where Horseshoe Mound is. It's that large horseshoe-shaped hill just east of town, around which U.S. Highway 20 winds before descending into Galena. Many are the weary travelers who rejoice when they round that curve and see the quaint houses and church steeples in the valley below.

Well, one day Bruce and his friend were coming around the mound on their way home. They had done it a hundred times before and nothing unusual had ever happened. But this time was incredibly different. As they rounded that curve, Bruce saw a human face and body materialize and hover outside the windshield of his car! It was not a distinct face--someone that they could identify--but it was definitely a human face. It had not only a head, but legs and arms; and it appeared to be sort of a smoky-gray color. It hovered in front of the windshield and then flew up over the car, disappearing as mysteriously as it had appeared!

Neither individual in the car knew if the other had seen the same thing, until one said to the other after a few moments: "Did you see that?" "Yes!" was the immediate response. Both had seen the very same thing. Neither had ever experienced such a thing, either before or since. And neither has an explanation.

Could Bruce and his friend have seen the railroad man, looking for his train? Or was it simply, as some might suggest, light reflecting off the windshield? You be the judge.

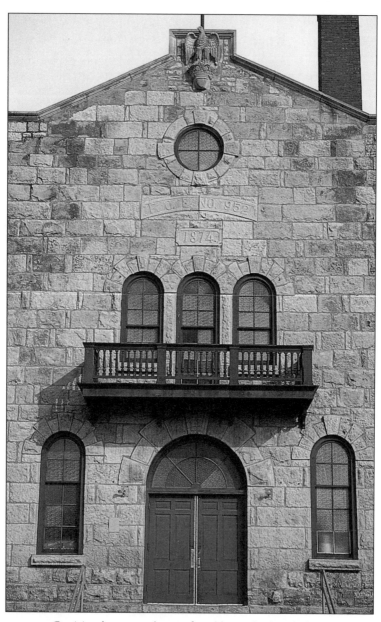

On March 14, 1910 he was found lying dead in the hall.

"THE GHOST OF TURNER HALL"

Turner Hall is a landmark for Galenians. It was constructed in 1874 by the Turner Society. Originating in Germany, the idea was to encourage "a sound mind in a sound body." Gymnastics, theater, literature--all were emphasized as the movement spread throughout German communities in America.

In Galena, the Turners succeeded in building a solid, stone structure designed for the "special use of the citizens of this city, without regard to politics, religion or nationality, as well as for entertainments of a respectable character."

Over the years Turner Hall has served politicians, bands, theater groups and various community organizations. It seems only natural that stories of ghosts would become a part of its character.

Ann, a volunteer at the hall, reports that many of those involved with the Save Turner Hall Fund, and others working to renovate the hall, have experienced strange things, including herself.

On one memorable occasion, she and fellow worker Kate were standing backstage near the back rock wall. Suddenly both felt as if they had just stepped into a tunnel of icy air. "What's that?" asked Kate. "I don't know," responded Ann, "but let's move!"

They immediately did. At that moment a small stone, which had come loose from way up in the loft, came crashing to the floor where they had just been standing! They were the only ones backstage. Was it coincidental? Or was Turner Hall's ghost trying to tell them something?

On another occasion, Ann and three others were standing inside the foyer area. They were getting ready to leave, being the last ones in the hall after a night of working on sets. Suddenly, all four became aware simultaneously that someone had just walked past one of the dressing room doors at the far end of the hall (both were closed at the time). Their collective response was: "Who is that?" (Not "What's that?" but "Who?") They all searched backstage, but found no one.

During other years there were many who reported cool drafts, lights being turned on and off and things turning up missing when no one was around. One person even brought in a medium from nearby Dubuque, Iowa, who thought she could see some type of spirit being in the balcony.

Most recently, Mike was in the hall when restoration work was going on. He had been up in the third floor attic area and came down the steps to leave, turning off the light switch as he passed. He turned, however, because something caught his eye. "Gee," he thought suddenly, "I just turned the light off on someone up there!" He was convinced that he had seen someone right before the light had gone off. A quick search, however, revealed not a soul.

Who, or what, is behind the "Ghost of Turner Hall?" Research into the past occupancy of the hall provided an answer for some. Charles Scheerer was the first manager of the building. He was part of the Scheerer, Armbruster & Coleman firm, dealers in all kinds of furniture, including coffins. Charles also helped with undertaking duties when called upon. Their firm was located next to Turner Hall and it was natural for Charles to look after things, particularly since he was also the Turner Society's treasurer.

Charles took care of the hall faithfully, even after his age restricted his activities. Finally, on March 14, 1910, he was found lying dead in the hall, apparently from natural causes. Those who believe in such things, however, feel that Charles is still watching over Turner Hall, making his presence known from time to time, as the need arises.

The voice was loud – and very angry!

"TURNER HALL REVISITED"

The Historical Society presented a program on the "Ghosts of Galena" during the spring of 1994. One of the sites visited in the presentation was Turner Hall. After the program, a local minister who had attended the presentation came up to visit. It turned out that he had a story of his own to tell about Turner Hall.

Three years earlier, he and his daughter were in the hall helping to set up for a "Ground Hog Dance," a fund raiser for Galena's Art and Recreation Center. Two workers had just left, leaving only the two of them. They were in the balcony putting a projector in place, the intent being to project the image of a ground hog onto a curtain behind the stage.

The work was about finished and they were ready to leave when both heard a male voice--quite loud and distinct-- coming from the north side of the balcony. It was localized in one area of the seats. They could not make out the words, but it sounded loud--and more importantly--very angry!

This went on for 15-20 seconds. When it quit, the minister's daughter asked, somewhat alarmed: "Did you hear that?" "Yes!" replied the father. But neither could imagine what it might be.

They quickly finished what they were doing. The minister tried to remain calm so that his daughter would not become more alarmed. He thought to himself that there must be some logical explanation--maybe someone was hurt, for example. He walked over to that area--timidly--and looked around. Nothing. Then, as they were leaving the balcony, they heard it again! Same sound, same angry tone! They quickly left but in doing so checked outside for a source to the sound. There was no explanation. To this day he wonders if a less than nice spirit had manifested itself to him, perhaps because he is a man of the cloth . . .

She saw him walking through
the sitting room.

"BRADNER SMITH VISITATIONS"

Richard and Zelma (their real names) live in the 1855 Bradner Smith House, one of the few in Galena with an original privy still attached. In this case it is a fine two-story privy on the back of the house, kept now strictly for aesthetic purposes.

Bradner Smith is said to have been a descendant of Cotton Mather Smith, the famous fire and brimstone New England preacher of three centuries ago. Bradner Smith came to Galena in the 1840s as a foreman carpenter, to oversee the construction of a stage coach barn for the Frink and Walker Stage Coach Company. In 1860 he listed himself in a local business directory simply as a "capitalist." He was a defendant in the famous Madison Y. Johnson lawsuit and contributed toward the purchase of the house presented to General U. S. Grant after the Civil War.

At the time of Mr. Smith's "manifestation" Richard was living and working as a cabinetmaker in Mr. Smith's house, with his workshop in the former kitchen. One day, while working on the reconstruction of some windows for the house, he was having a difficult time fitting the mullions in place, although this would surely have been a routine task for any apprentice in Smith's day.

Richard's temper was not improved when he suddenly sensed a somewhat amused and perhaps slightly impatient presence saying "Man, you're making an awfully hard job of that!"

The message, if that's what it was, was specifically sensed, rather than heard. It certainly came "out of the blue," since Richard was totally preoccupied with his own problems, and wasn't thinking of Bradner Smith or anyone else. Furthermore, based on what historical evidence exists, he suspects Mr. Smith was far too dignified and conscious of his own importance to have any truck with "ghostly assistance." Far more likely he was, and perhaps still is, keeping an eye on his house, and the communication was more an irresistible outbreak of exasperation on seeing a simple job bungled than any thought of help from the spirit world.

A different visitant may have appeared when Richard's mother was visiting. She had never met either Bernie or Mary Eberhardt, the elderly couple and immediately previous owners from whom Richard and Zelma bought Mr. Smith's house.

It was a pleasant Saturday afternoon, and Richard's mother was relaxing in the upstairs sitting room. While she was resting there, as she described it later, an elderly man quietly walked into the room and proceeded through to the back bedroom beyond. Although normally rather excitable, she apparently accepted the "visitor" without either question or comment and, highly uncharacteristically, did not mention the incident to either Richard or Zelma.

On Sunday, a neighbor stopped over to convey the news that Bernie Eberhardt had died the day before in California. On hearing this news, Richard's mother asked if Mr. Eberhardt was a tall, thin man who generally needed a shave. She then proceeded, quite unprompted, to describe Mr. Eberhardt's appearance in accurate and exact detail, right down to the color of eyes and the pattern of his coat.

Since she had never seen so much as a picture of Mr. Eberhardt, they asked how she could describe him so accurately. She then said that she saw him walking through the sitting room the previous day.

Rather plaintively she commented, "I don't see why he was wearing an overcoat on a hot July day like yesterday."

Richard remembered that the Eberhardts had said that the back bedroom was Bernie's favorite room in the house. In fact, in their courting days when Bernie came calling on Mary Cloren (the Cloren family bought the house from Bradner Smith's estate) he would occasionally stay overnight in the back bedroom if inclement weather made the several mile country walk back to the Eberhardt home look too grim.

On another occasion, Richard saw something he could not logically explain. He was alone, relaxing in the quiet of the evening in the tiny garden beside Mr. Smith's house. Tucked between two houses at a slightly lower level, the garden is filled with ferns, intersected with graveled paths, and is quite secluded in spite of being in the middle of town.

Just this once, on this utterly still, warm summer evening, Richard noticed the ferns edging the path move gently. It was exactly as though a lady had entered at the gate and walked past the fountain to the front of the garden, her long skirt brushing the ferns as she passed. There was no wind, and none of the ferns except those bordering the path moved.

Richard has no explanation--except for Miss Emily Smith, an obviously beloved niece of Bradner's who lived in the house until she married that rising young lawyer/soldier John A. Rawlins. She died, tragically, of tuberculosis only a few years later. Her husband went on to become U.S. Grant's Chief of Staff during the Civil War and then his Secretary of War in 1869; only to die of tuberculosis a few months later.

As she watched, the boy raised the object.

"THE INDIAN BOY"

Nestled alongside one of the quaintest streets in our town is a delightful little cottage constructed over 150 years ago. The owners love their home and would never trade it for anything. They did, however, have a tale to tell after first moving in.

One night shortly after Catherine and Jim purchased the home, they had retired to the little bedroom on the first floor (the stone portion). This lower section of the home is reached by a small but very steep flight of steps. In fact, they are almost ladder-like. Soon they were fast asleep when Catherine suddenly awoke--hearing what sounded like bare feet coming down the steep steps. She looked over to see in the dim light what appeared to be the figure of a young adolescent Indian.

This was not your typical North American Indian, but rather one with features more Central or South American. He had long black hair, bronze skin, and was of a very petite and fine-boned stature. His lightweight, simple garment was light-colored, and he appeared to be wearing a small head-covering, but Catherine wasn't sure.

She was more certain, however, about the object which he held in his hands. It was a box-like object which she feared was some type of blow-gun. As she watched, the boy raised the object.

Catherine's first thought was that he was going to blow something at her. In fear, she turned over and put her arm over her husband--an almost instinctive reaction. But as Catherine did so, she thought: "What if this is not a weapon--maybe it's a musical instrument . . ." She then turned back to look once again, but the boy was gone! By this time she was sitting bolt upright and trembling, the experience having been so real. Meanwhile, her husband, Jim, slept through the entire episode!

Several times thereafter, Catherine had the feeling of someone or something--a presence--being in the "stone room." She felt no more fear, however, and the feeling faded. Since that time Catherine has experienced nothing more out of the ordinary.

"GUEST PRESENCE"

Ed and Amy fell in love with Galena while on a visit from the suburban Chicago area. They wanted to become a part of the community, even though Ed's business would keep at least one of them in the "City" for several more years. They purchased a large, turn-of-the-century two-story brick home that had not been lived in for many years. It needed a tremendous amount of work, but they were willing. They began by virtually gutting the house. It was during this time that they first noticed something unusual.

At one end of the dining room were two large swinging doors. The hinges were rusty and they would not swing well. When Ed and Amy left after a weekend of work, the doors would be left shut. Imagine their surprise when, upon returning the next week, one of the doors was found in an open position! The house was locked, no one was inside, and nothing else had been touched. Ed, however, was (and is) a nonbeliever and could always explain the phenomenon through some rational explanation.

Amy, however, wasn't so sure. She later noticed their dog Maggie roaming from room to room, simply unable to settle down. This was very uncharacteristic behavior.

The renovation work went well, however, and soon the house was ready. One afternoon, soon after moving in, Amy was going up the stairs when she stopped suddenly. She could definitely hear men's voices coming from one of the bedrooms, but no one else was supposed to be in the house. She quickly checked to make sure, but not a soul was to be found.

Amy began to call their "visitor" John Gardner, first resident after whom the home was named. It was about this time that she was out in the kitchen working when suddenly-- with no warning--a cookbook literally flew off the shelf and fell to the floor. Amy and her two pets--a dog and a cat--all hovered together for a moment, each as startled as the other!

While this first episode was quite a shock, Amy adjusted, for over the next few months the same thing happened several more times--always the same shelf and the same cookbook.

Amy also noticed little things turning up missing, only to be found much later. They are the kinds of things you would think had simply been misplaced . . . only Amy knew better. She even got to the point where she'd say: "John Gardner--Knock it off!"

The cookbook literally flew off the shelf . . .

Because they have a guest house, Amy and Ed do not bother guests with tales of ghostly presences. It was with much surprise, then, that guests one morning asked: "Does John Gardner come by very often?" They had been sitting on the porch swing the previous afternoon and had turned to see a man walking through the dining room. But there was absolutely no one in the house!

More recently, both Amy and Ed have heard yet one more thing to make them wonder. Their bedroom is on the third floor, but one night both distinctly heard those dining room doors swinging. Again, they were the only ones in the house!

Things have settled down, now, at Ed and Amy's house. Little unusual has happened recently. Ed remains a nonbeliever, but not Amy. She remains convinced that someone else is still there.

Just a friendly ghost sampling the spirits.

"REFRESHING SPIRITS"

In 1964 Tom and Wendy purchased a fine old duplex on one of Galena's oldest streets. The house was in ill repair and they found themselves redoing the wiring, plumbing, and heating. But it was worth it. The house has three floors: the basement level with its recreation room; the first floor with its living room, family/dining room and kitchen; an open staircase leading to the second floor with its bath, three bedrooms and a sun porch off the master bedroom; and finally, another open staircase leading to the third floor with two additional bedrooms.

When Tom and Wendy first moved in, they had a two year old daughter named Heather. They lived in the house from August of 1964 to December of that year with no unusual happenings. Then one evening in December they were lying in bed when they heard footsteps walking above them on the third floor. They went to investigate but found no one.

They returned to their bedroom only to have the footsteps start up again. This became a regular occurrence. The family had the room checked for loose boards, windows that could rattle and anything else that might explain the footsteps. They found no answer.

At this point the family accepted the fact that their house must be haunted. Wendy noted that she was a person frightened of her own shadow, yet this "ghost" never made her feel unsafe.

In 1969 more strange things began to happen. Tom came home from work and parked his car across the street from the house. It was late at night and he noted that the light was on in the sun porch. When he entered the house and found his daughters and wife watching T.V. he reminded them that they had left the light on.

Wendy told him, however, that both she and the girls had just arrived home and had not been to the second floor. Tom then went to the second floor only to find that the light had been turned off! The problem with the lights continued. The family called in electricians to see if there was a wiring problem. There was not.

In 1970 with their younger daughter Lisa in preschool and their older daughter in kindergarten, Wendy decided to get a part-time job. She worked in the afternoon while the girls were in school. She was very meticulous about making the beds every day before she went to work. One day she came home from work and went upstairs to her bedroom to change clothes and found that the bed had been turned down--just like a maid would do it. Wendy had no explanation since neither she nor the girls had been in the house since the bed was made. These episodes continued for over a month!

Friends suggested that possibly the family's two French poodles were responsible. "This is not possible," Wendy would reply, "because when the family is not at home the poodles are closed in the kitchen with a four-foot gate. There is no way small toy poodles could jump over the gate."

In 1971 the family planned a vacation out west. Tom wanted to take some cash along in addition to travelers checks. He went to the bank the night before and got $300 in cash. He returned home and put the cash in plain sight on top of the stereo in the living room. The entire family left the house the next morning for their vacation.

About 100 miles from home, Tom asked Wendy if she had picked up the money. She had not. They were too far from home to return, so continued on their two-week journey.

Their house was secure, for when they purchased the home, Tom changed all of the locks on the doors, so that no previous owner would have a key. Before leaving on the vacation, he also checked all the windows (on which he had installed additional latches) and doors to make sure they were locked.

When the family returned from vacation the house was still secure. There was no sign of forced entry. When they entered the living room, however, they found an empty bottle of liquor (which had been in the bar in the basement) sitting on the coffee table! In the kitchen they found two glasses washed and placed in the dish rack to dry! The money was still sitting on the stereo in plain sight. There were numerous antiques and pieces of good jewelry in the house. Nothing had been touched. A break-in? They suspected not. It was, they're convinced, just their friendly ghost, checking out the spirits.

It's the little things that make you wonder.

"DON'T BLAME THE DOG!"

It was in July of 1992 that Bill purchased and moved into a very quaint and historic cottage on one of Galena's older streets. The original part of the house was constructed in 1836 and various alterations had been made by many families over the years.

Bill was very comfortable with the house except for one thing: lights kept coming on by themselves. He would leave for work and everything would be shut off. Upon his return, however, he would find a basement light--or some other light--shining brightly.

At first he blamed it on being new to the house. Maybe he didn't know how all the switches worked, or possibly there was an electrical problem. But he made a special effort to be careful--to turn everything off when he left--all to no avail.

The bathroom light was a case in point. It was wired to a dimmer switch on the wall. Because of his dog, Bill liked to leave the switch on dim so the animal could see her way around at night while he was out. Imagine his surprise when he came home to find the light on the bright setting. When asked if the dog could have adjusted the dimmer switch Bill replied: "No way, it was not the dog."

There were other things. Out of the corner of his eye, Bill would sometimes see shadows move in front of windows, especially the dining room and kitchen windows. It was never anything identifiable, for the minute you looked again, it was gone. After Bill had lived in the house for a while, things quieted down. In fact, everything seemed normal.

Then, in July of 1994, Bill's girlfriend and her daughter moved in. Things began to happen again almost immediately. The answering machine, for example, began turning itself on.

Sometimes objects would fall or tip over on the kitchen counter for no apparent reason. One morning Bill's girlfriend was coming down the stairs and felt someone tap her on the shoulder! She also felt little blasts of cold air. This was more than a little unnerving since no one else was near. On another occasion she was taking a shower when a sudden blast of cold water--immediately followed by warm-- sprayed from the shower head. No one else in the house was using any water.

"Since there is no exhaust fan in the bathroom," Bill said, "we always open a window when the shower is used to let the steam out." One day he opened the window and took a shower. But upon finishing, the window was closed. "The window," continued Bill, "is located in the shower stall, works hard--it sticks--and could not have closed by itself."

Another puzzling incident happened one evening as Bill walked from the kitchen through the dining room. He noticed a rather large wet spot on an area rug in the middle of the room. "It was odd," Bill said, "because two edges of the carpet were also wet, but the carpet was still dry between the spot and the edges."

There was also moisture trailing off to a hole in the floor, following the slant of the floor. From there it had dripped into the basement where it seemed to have evaporated. The dog was outside so Bill knew that it wasn't her fault.

"Where did the water come from," Bill wondered. "There is no plumbing or water pipes in this part of the house, and nothing was spilled upstairs in the room above. Weird!"

Now, any one of these things by themselves would not cause anyone to think twice, but when added up over time, even the skeptic might wonder. Bill has yet to collect all of the history on the house, but when he does, he hopes to find a clue to the many little things he can't explain.

"A strong gust of cold air was directed into my face . . ."

"BREAKING GLASS AND GUSTS OF AIR"

Harold lives in a cozy little stone cottage up on the hill. It was built in 1852 by a German stonemason and has served its occupants well ever since. Harold agreed to share the following with us. Interestingly, he reports that his strange visitations ceased when he married and his wife moved in . . .

"On three separate occasions, sometimes a year or two apart, while spending an evening reading in my study, the silence would be shattered by the distinct sound of breaking glass. The sound was always directed from the rear of the house, and resembled someone holding a glass globe high above their head . . . and then dropping it upon the floor. I would bolt from my chair to check the 'damage', fully expecting that someone had tossed a brick through the rear window . . . but upon investigation, would find NOTHING.

On another occasion, at about the time of one of the aforementioned incidents, I had just turned out the light and settled into bed when a strong gust of cold air was directed into my face . . . no windows open, no furnace or air conditioner in operation. My initial thought was that there was a bat flying about the room . . . and that it had passed close to my face creating the 'wind'. I turned on the light and searched the room . . . peering behind all the curtains in search of the furry beast . . . but again NOTHING."

Something was causing the pictures to tilt . . .

"O.C. WELCH AND FAMILY"

Robert and Elizabeth own one of our favorite Galena homes. Perched high atop the hills, it provides a splendid view of the neighborhood. The original stone section may have been constructed in 1828, according to their research. The main house is of the Federal style and was built in 1845 of Galena brick. There have been no significant alterations since, and surprisingly, the house was inhabited by the same old Irish family for seven generations. The first significant change was with the entrance of Robert and Elizabeth.

Robert says that he is basically a nonbeliever in ghosts, but right after they purchased and started work on their house, he really did begin to wonder. Doors that had been left open would be found closed or vice versa. Windows would be found open, too, but as Robert observed, this could simply have been counterweights causing the problem.

Once moved in, however, they began to notice that pictures hung straight would be askew when they returned after a week in suburban Chicago. They would carefully straighten them, only to have them tilted upon their return. Some of these pictures were very solidly affixed to the wall. The chance of traffic causing the house to shake and jar the pictures seemed remote. As Robert puts it: "The house is well above the street and is built on solid bedrock--nothing shakes it."

An even more extreme example occurred three years ago right before Christmas. The central stairway has family photos of Robert's on one side and of Elizabeth's on the other. On this occasion, Elizabeth's mother was staying with them and was using an upstairs bedroom. Upon coming downstairs, she noticed that a favorite picture of Elizabeth's--showing two aunts as young girls sitting on the lap of Santa Claus--was hanging upside down. The picture was out of reach and could not have just tilted. To this day they do not have an explanation. But other strange things continued to happen.

Robert's son took a picture of the house with a telephoto lens from across the valley. Upon getting the picture back, he found what appears to be a figure standing in one of the windows. On another occasion, two summers ago, Robert and Elizabeth were working in the yard and heard someone tapping on the window glass of the parlor. A quick search found no one in--or even near--the house.

It was after this that Richard was buying a gift in a shop downtown. He was thrilled to find the clerk had lived in the house as a young child. She and her sister often listened to voices in the wall at night! That's how they went to sleep, he was told, listening to the voices with their ears pressed against the wall!

On another occasion, Robert and Elizabeth had a harpist staying at the home. After returning from an engagement at Eagle Ridge, she was eating a late snack and became aware of a distant, but distinct, conversation. It sounded as if it was coming from upstairs. It was not a radio. She experienced this same thing several times while staying at the house. She was, prior to this time, unaware of any ghost stories about the house.

Two Christmases ago, Robert and Elizabeth had family visiting and had pulled out Robert's old Lionel train set for some of the kids to play with. He restricted them to two cars maximum because of the wear on the old train set. That

is the way they left the set when everyone went to bed. But the next morning, they found all the cars attached to the train engine. Not only that, but Elizabeth's brother, a man in his 40s, swore that he had heard the train set running in the middle of the night. In fact, he had gotten out of bed and checked the rooms to find where the sound was coming from. He also checked on the kids, who were all sound asleep.

The ballot box had its own story to tell.

And then there's the ballot box affair . . . Robert had purchased an early (1920s) ballot box which used marbles for the voting. It was used by various types of organizations for admitting new members or deciding other issues of the day. As the box was passed around to the members, an individual would take a marble out of the open side and drop it through a small hole on the covered half. All the marbles were white, except one, which was black. If someone picked up the black marble and dropped it through the hole, then whoever was trying to gain admission to that organization was "blackballed," thus the origin of the term.

Robert brought his new find home and displayed it as a conversation piece. His curiosity was aroused, however, when after being gone for a period of time, he would return to find the marbles in the box rearranged. Sometimes they would be in the shape of a number, or letter. At other times there would be no pattern at all. After a time, Elizabeth determined to copy down on paper each different arrangement found. "What if they were messages?" she wondered. The mystery continues.

A stranger story came from an older lady, unaware of the home's ghost stories, who was visiting from Minneapolis. She had lost most of her eyesight six or seven years previously and had developed her other senses to a much greater degree. She stayed overnight in the back bedroom. The next morning, at breakfast, she calmly asked: "Do you know that you have three spirits in your house?"

She then described them as two small children and a third, very shy, withdrawn spirit who was an adult. She had seen them the previous night. The two children were standing at the foot of her bed staring at her, while the third spirit hid in the shadows, not wanting to be seen. She was of the opinion that they were all quite harmless, simply curious.

Through historical research, Robert and Elizabeth had found that O.C. Welch (who had built the Federal portion of the house in 1845) and two of his children had died in the house. The obituary described his death in some detail, for he had climbed out of bed at 4 o'clock on a January morning but fell to the floor with a loud crash, perhaps from a heart attack. The noise was loud enough to wake his son in one of the adjacent bedrooms.

This brings us to the mantel clock. One night both Robert and Elizabeth were awakened by a large bang downstairs in the living room. In that room was a large, upright clock sitting on the mantel over the old fireplace. Upon investigation, they found that the clock, which had been in excellent working order, had stopped. The heavy

It was 4 A.M., the exact time of death for O.C. Welch.

nylon cord holding the counterweight had been severed--and the falling weight had caused the noise. How the heavy cord had been severed could not be answered. But even more bizarre was the hour that the clock had stopped. It was 4 A.M., the exact time of death for O.C. Welch! And then Robert and Elizabeth realized something even more incredible. The clock had also stopped on the same day of the month that O.C. Welch had died!

There have been other incidents, as well. Recently Robert and Elizabeth went downtown for some things and left the radio on. It was a classical music station which they frequently listen to. Imagine their surprise, when upon return, they heard the radio blaring rock music. A quick check of the dial revealed that it was nowhere near the proper setting. Thus, a change in reception did not cause the original station to fade. They are convinced that no one had entered the house in their absence.

Another incident was not like the others. Elizabeth had gone to bed early and was trying to fall asleep, but was being kept awake by the antics of Robert. She told him to stop rubbing her leg, talking and annoying her. He would, as he often does, tease her with: "How you doing, sweety girl?"

And then he'd giggle. Finally, Elizabeth got tired of this and went downstairs--only to find Robert coming in the back door from running errands. Had she been dreaming? Elizabeth doesn't think so, given their many other experiences with the house.

One night recently, Robert awoke in the middle of the night because he heard whispering very close by. It was as if someone was leaning over whispering right into his ear. He sat up and it stopped. Elizabeth was asleep and Robert chose not to say anything then, but he did a few days later. A strange look came over her face as she said "I experienced the same thing the night before."

On yet another night, Elizabeth awoke to see a very bright triangle of light on the wall across the room. It had very sharp edges and was very distinct. She became alarmed. It was extremely bright, yet no other lights were on and no reflection could explain it. Elizabeth stared at it for a good 10-15 seconds. "Oh my God, this is not possible!" she thought. But then it began to fade. She immediately awoke her husband: "Did you see that, Robert?" She was extremely upset. Robert, however, saw nothing. The mystery only deepened when, on another occasion, a guest staying in another bedroom told of seeing the same bright light!

Robert and Elizabeth continue to enjoy their house. The strange things they've described may or may not have an explanation. They don't seem to mind, however. It's all part of the experience of living in a wonderful old home.

Who was the woman on the stairway?

"A GUEST HOUSE WITH UNINVITED GUESTS"

In 1990, Bonnie and her husband Don purchased a beautiful historic home for a bed & breakfast establishment. Initially, Bonnie's husband was only in Galena on weekends but she was able to be there full time. About two months after she had moved in, Bonnie, her daughter and three small children were alone in the house. It was late in the evening and the kids were upstairs sleeping.

Suddenly, Bonnie and her daughter heard footsteps upstairs in the hallway. They naturally assumed that one of the kids was up, but when they went up to check, all three were sound asleep in their beds. They returned downstairs, only to hear the footsteps again. Another hurried trip upstairs revealed nothing--all the kids were fast asleep.

They thought it curious, but were new to the house and realized that it takes a while to get used to the various sounds that an older house can make. It was with some surprise, then, when later that night they heard voices. It was a man and a woman talking--they couldn't make out the words but the sound was otherwise quite distinct. They looked upstairs to see if someone was up there. No one. They looked downstairs. No one. They then turned on all the lights on the outside of the house thinking perhaps someone was outside the house talking. Nothing. The voices continued, however, for at least thirty minutes!

Then, last year in March, another episode came to pass. Shortly before this, Bonnie and her husband had reopened the original basement stairway immediately below the main stairway leading to the second floor. This had been sealed off and enclosed many years previously and the space used as a closet.

It was late, her husband was already upstairs sleeping and Bonnie was going around turning off lights and locking up for the night. The only lights still on were little electric candle lights in the window that were left on all the time. As Bonnie walked past the "new" basement stairway she suddenly froze. There was a woman walking up from the basement!

It was a woman who appeared to be 40-50 years of age. Bonnie could clearly make her out from the window lights still on. The sight was all the more startling because the woman was dressed in 19th century period clothing. She wore a brown and white gingham check dress. Her hair--in fact everything about her--was definitely 19th century. At this point Bonnie caught herself, blinked, and looked twice, but the woman was gone! She had disappeared into thin air!

That was not the end of strange visitations. Recently,

Bonnie was up late one evening reading. Her husband had already retired to the upstairs. Suddenly, she became aware of voices. She could not tell exactly where they came from, but got up and wandered through the house listening. With no luck downstairs, she went upstairs and walked into the back hall of the house. The voices had ceased by this time, but she was startled to smell the unmistakable odor of pipe smoke. Now, both Bonnie and her husband are cigarette smokers, but pipe smokers--never! Again, there was absolutely no one else in the house.

Exactly one week later, Bonnie was again reading late, as she likes to do, but this time she heard a door slam. Being the only one around, she again searched the house to see what door was closed that shouldn't have been. And once again, when she reached the back hall upstairs, she was confronted by the same aromatic pipe smoke. And again, not a pipe-smoking soul was to be found . . .

Hovering over her bed was an apparition.

"NUNS AND VOICES"

Margaret is basically a nonbeliever in ghosts, but her experiences with ownership of a fine old guest house left her wondering. The first episode occurred on the night of October 22, 1989. Margaret had rented the small guest room in the southeast corner of the second floor to Kirsten. Kirsten retired in the evening, but awoke in the middle of the night to something she had never expected. Hovering over her was an apparition of what looked like a nun. The woman was seen near the door and appeared non-threatening.

Kirsten lay there, uncertain of what was happening. As

she watched, however, the nun smiled at her and was gone. Kirsten thought she was dreaming, but just to make certain, she jumped out of bed and stood straight up! She was definitely not dreaming. Margaret, upon hearing the tale next morning, paid little attention and said nothing to any subsequent guests.

A few months later, another individual was renting the same room. Nancy had no knowledge of Kirsten or of her strange experience in that room. Nor had Margaret said anything to her about it. Awakening in the middle of the night, however, Nancy saw a woman hovering over her! She described the woman as having some type of cover or veil over her face. Again, the woman gently smiled and then disappeared. Both apparitions had appeared in the same place--over the bed and near the door to the room. Was it coincidental?

Margaret subsequently redecorated the room. A door was closed up, furniture rearranged, and new wallpaper put up. Since that time, no one has experienced any more visitations in that room.

Margaret did report later, however, that she and at least one other individual heard sounds like murmuring voices in the wall. She heard those voices more than once--always men--always in the living room area. On two occasions, she walked down the stairway listening to the voices, but they stopped upon her reaching the bottom.

On another occasion, a guest added to the mystery. "Who was that talking downstairs at three this morning," she asked. Margaret's daughter, it turned out, had also heard the same thing. She didn't want to say anything to her mother, however, for fear of scaring her.

The explanation for those voices, some say, could be wind circulating down the old chimney that serves the parlor fireplace. Maybe. Whatever the case, nothing more has been heard since.

"I told you, I'm upstairs!"

"BAGPIPES A PLAYING"

Our next "ghost site" is a simple but elegant structure constructed of Galena brick in the 1840s. It was once the home of a Civil War general. Shirley moved in during 1979. Her mother-in-law, helping her move, was up on the third floor putting things away. Shirley had just come up to the second floor when she heard her mother-in-law shout: "I told you, I'm upstairs!" Shirley thought this odd since she had not called her. Upon checking, she found that her mother-in-law was responding for the third time! Though no one was in the house, the woman distinctly heard someone ask three times where she was. Shirley, being the only other person around, had heard nothing.

Things settled down and Shirley experienced nothing more until the night of the bagpipes. She sleeps on the second floor, and this night was awakened by the noise of bagpipes, or at least something sounding very similar. She quietly got up and searched the house from top to bottom. She could not find the source; the sound meanwhile had ceased.

Puzzled, Shirley returned to bed, but no sooner had she done so than once again the strange sound returned. This time, more annoyed than anything, she sat up and said: "Hey, don't do that when I'm trying to sleep!" The sound stopped and Shirley heard nothing more that night. In fact, she heard nothing more for a period of several months. On occasion, the sound is still heard, but Shirley just talks to it and says, "Hey, I'm tired and want to go to bed. Let me sleep." And it does.

Shirley has noticed one other thing as well. She likes to read in the parlor, and it is there that she feels a presence at times. Interestingly, her pets never go into the parlor--it's the only room in the house that they shy away from. Despite these oddities, Shirley could not be happier with her house.

Leslie's father was not amused by his
son's invention of a glass casket.

"LESLIE"

Galena has many fine old mansions. Some, however, seem to attract more attention than others. This particular home has spawned stories of ghosts for many years, through a succession of owners. A typical episode occurred in 1982 when a travel writer was staying at the home.

It was a night with low, threatening clouds, gusty winds and a sense of "anticipation." The beautiful French doors to the balcony were carefully locked as our guest retired for the evening. Hours later, she awoke with a start. A cold wind was gushing through those French doors, which were now wide open!

The next morning she told of her experience, suggesting

that someone must have been in her room and unlocked those doors. Everyone assured her, however, that no one had been near her room. No one could explain, though, how the doors could have come open.

Over the years, individuals working at the house have experienced similar mysteries. Perhaps the most annoying of these has been finding doors and windows unlocked when they had been left locked or vice versa. The phenomenon seemed particularly acute on the third floor. It was quite unnerving for some, and no one seemed to be responsible.

On one occasion, a worker heard a large crash and ran into another room only to find that a large painting had fallen from the wall. Somehow, a chair was involved, for it's legs were poking through the painting. On quieter occasions, the help would notice pets acting strangely. There was, for example, the cat purring on the stairway, acting as if someone were petting it.

Our first knowledge of the home's spirit came when one of us ran into Marsha, who served as a tour guide at the home. She was out sweeping in front of her house and something was obviously on her mind. It seems that she had just returned from a rather unsettling experience at the home.

It was the end of the day and she and another girl were locking up. It was one of those very hot and humid summer days, and the windows of the cupola three floors up had been opened for ventilation. The girls were just locking the front door when they realized that those windows had not been closed. Marsha ran up to close them while her friend waited on the front porch.

She wound her way up the steps to the very top. She was about to close and latch a window but stopped momentarily to admire from her dizzying perch the view across the town. Suddenly, despite the sultry heat of the afternoon, she felt a draft of cold air envelop her! And then Marsha felt something more--she described it like "someone's hand"--

pressing against her back! It literally pushed her toward the window! For an instant she froze.

Marsha still doesn't know if something actually pushed her or if she was instinctively responding to the chill that had enveloped her. Never-the-less, she whirled around to see who was behind her, thinking momentarily that her co-worker was playing some kind of trick. No one was there, yet she continued to feel the icy chill of the air around her.

In a panic, she tore down three flights of stairs and raced out the front door. Her co-worker was there waiting but could.hardly understand what all the commotion was about.

Marsha refused to go back up for those windows, so her co-worker did, carefully looking about as she worked her way up. Once up to the cupola, she found everything in order. No chilly draft, no strange feelings, nothing. She closed and latched the windows and left.

Over the years others had reported hearing footsteps and also of feeling those bone-chilling drafts, but no one could offer any explanation . . . other than the story of Lester.

Lester was supposedly the young son of one of the early owners of the house. The story relates that, one day when alone, Lester found his way to the third floor and climbed into a large, ornately carved coffin. The lid closed and latched, and the boy suffocated.

At the museum, we tried to verify this story but found insufficient evidence to either support or refute it. We did find, however, a newspaper clipping that identified the third owner of the home as Madison Y. Johnson, a controversial and cantankerous lawyer heavily involved in Galena politics. Johnson had an adult, unmarried son, Leslie, who lived reclusively in the home with his mother. Imagine our surprise when we learned from the clipping that Leslie invented, among other things, a solid glass coffin! (This coffin was said to have been on display for a short while in the Smithsonian Institute.)

A newspaper reporter in 1883 caught up with Leslie and filed this report for his *Galena Daily Gazette* (June 14) readers:

"GLASS BURIAL CASKET"

"Invention of a Galena Boy, Which Promises to Supplant the Present Unsatisfactory System of Burying the Dead--A Receptacle Which Completely Mummifies Bodies Placed Therein-- The Discoverer Interviewed.

Reporter--I understand that the Government has just granted you a patent for a glass burial casket and basket to protect it, which is said to possess numberless advantages over the present system of burying the dead?

Mr. Johnson--Yes, such a patent has been received by me, and if all they say about it is true, we are getting back to the days of the Pharaohs, and will be able to leave to the world our own mummies, as they did in ancient days.

Reporter--As it is now public and protected by patent, will you please inform me, for the enlightenment of the readers of the Gazette, how you came to make the discovery, and explain it's advantages?

Mr. Johnson--. . . I was led into searching for some substance in which bodies could be deposited without danger of contagion or infection from exposure, and as a further means of forever preventing decay. Investigation and experiment led me to adopt glass, as not being liable to decay or destructability from the atmosphere or contact with the earth or other substance. The casket, for which I hold a patent, is hermetically sealed; and to protect it from all injury, I have invented an iron basket to hold it intact, with handles attached, so that it can be carried with perfect ease.

Reporter--What are the advantages of a glass casket?

Mr. Johnson--There are many. First, it is indestructable, as it will neither rust nor decay. Second, it can be hermetically sealed. Third, by introducing carbonic acid gas, from it's density the air would escape, and when hermetically sealed, the body would be preserved, as if embalmed, from decay. Fourth, it renders cremation unnecessary. Fifth, as a sanitary means, it would be adopted by cities to prevent the spread of contagion from decomposed bodies in transit to the burial place; but the most important advantage to my mind is, that it satisfies the sentiment and feelings of a Christian people that by it the dead are forever preserved from decomposition.

Reporter--How is it as regards expense?

Mr. Johnson--The cheaper casket would not cost more than the ordinary kind now in use, but you could make them as costly as desired. There is nothing on which you could display taste and expense more lavishly.

Reporter--Is there not danger of breakage or cracking in handling?

Mr. Johnson--Not the least, as it is protected by the iron basket, and covered both on the inside and outside with cloth cemented to the glass, which makes it's resistance almost equal to iron, and in passing through doors or other narrow passages, it could be handled as well by the ends as the sides, as the railing extends entirely around, making convenient handles on all sides, thereby lessening the danger of dropping, and at the same time protecting it."

How successful Leslie Johnson was with his glass coffin we can't say. We do know, though, that he had his laboratory and workshop in the house, and evidently pursued other inventions as well.

A few years later, his father died. While we are uncertain if the father was buried in a glass casket, we do know that his will expressly forbid his three children from receiving any inheritance until they married and had children of their own!

The home changed hands several times after the Johnsons. Exactly when the tales of hauntings began, we can't say. But while the home was reportedly haunted for many years, nothing of note has happened recently. Those familiar with the home feel that the trapped spirit--or whatever it was--has now departed to other places.

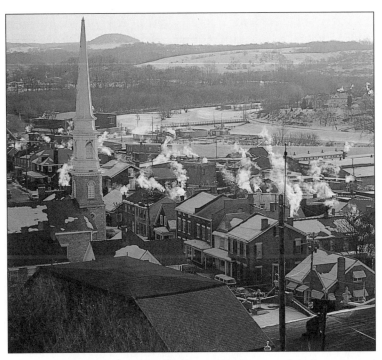

"You just know something — or someone — is there."

"THE MAN IN THE BROWN SUIT"

Dave and Laura lived in their apartment from 1980 to 1985. They had a three level unit with the bedroom located in what used to be the attic of one of Galena's large old buildings. They were the first people to live in that apartment after the structure was completely renovated.

Laura's first encounter came one day while lying on the couch in the living room. She'd stopped work for a breather and was just relaxing. Suddenly, she felt a presence over her and looked up to see a man standing there. He was, of all things, shaking a finger at her. She specifically remembers his brown suit and high-necked, starched white shirt. She was not really scared and felt his presence as much as saw it. He faded as quietly as he had appeared.

After that incident, Laura would hear sounds up in the bedroom which she couldn't quite identify. She felt on more than one occasion that there was a presence in the room. "It's a hard feeling to describe," she says. "You just know something--or someone--is there."

One night Laura was in bed lying on her stomach when she became aware that someone was in the room. She wondered what Dave was doing home, since he was not expected until later. To see if it was, indeed, her husband, she began to roll over, but felt the presence over her even more strongly than before. In fact, it was almost as if it were holding her down, for she could not turn completely over onto her back. Finally, she simply blurted out: "Leave me alone!" Almost immediately, she was freed.

Laura now realized that her husband had not returned, as she had first thought. There was no one there but her. She never truly felt threatened during any of her experiences, but it did make her wonder. Whatever the case, subsequent residents have experienced nothing unusual.

"It still feels as though someone else lives there."

"FOOTSTEPS IN THE NIGHT"

Jeffrey and Donna Meeker have been at their residence since 1985. Their daughter, Martha, was 15 when they moved in. Their home has been added onto over the years, but the original brick section was built in the 1850s. Initially, Donna was not working and shared the house with their two cats, "JB" and "Tuffy". She felt as though there was some type of presence in the house, but not a bad one. The family hadn't really talked about it, but about a year and a half after moving in, they sat down together and compared notes, so to speak.

Martha told of awakening one night and hearing what sounded like a toddler stumbling along the floor only to fall, landing on the rump as toddlers so often do. Martha had heard this more than once but wasn't particularly alarmed by it. Then one night she awoke and saw something on the floor. She thought it was one of the cats, but neither was in the room. She wondered if it was just her, or if the others were seeing and hearing things, too.

Then Jeffrey, the father, recalled footsteps he had heard one night. A thorough skeptic, he thought at first that the cats were acting up. But when he got up to investigate, the suspect felines were both sleeping. He stood in the doorway and continued hearing the steps. "That's strange!" he thought. The sounds seemed to be moving around the rooms, until finally they seemed to pass right through him! He could not explain it.

Jeffrey remained a nonbeliever, but Donna believed a ghost might be responsible. She began to do research. She found the first family who lived in the home was buried at Greenwood Cemetery in Galena. William Etherly lived in the house and his wife died in childbirth as did the child-- this around the turn-of-the-century.

Donna is convinced that the sounds they heard and the presences they felt were Mrs. Etherly and her lost child. She reports that after this research, no one in the house has heard or seen anything more. "But it still feels," she says, "as though someone else lives here."

*He used to joke about coming back to
haunt the place.*

"THE HUSBAND WHO
WOULDN'T LEAVE"

Susan had never worried much about ghosts. Neither she
nor her husband had ever experienced anything unusual in
their home located on a quiet street at the edge of town.
About the only time they talked about hauntings was when
her husband, Joe, joked about coming back to haunt her
after his death. He was not in good health and passed away a
short time later. It was then, and only then, that things began
to happen.

One morning Susan came downstairs to find the egg timer sitting right in the middle of their kitchen ledge. Now, there was nothing particularly wrong with this, except that her husband was the only one in the family that had ever used that egg timer, and it was never left on the ledge. He always put it back by the micro-wave, which is exactly where it had been the day before. No one else had been in the house and Susan knew that she had not touched it.

And so began a series of little mischievous things that could not readily be explained. On another occasion, Susan found some of her rings missing. She was fond of wearing five little rings. Each night, before retiring to the upstairs bedroom, she would remove the rings and place them in a small bowl. But on this particular morning she came down to find the bowl with only two rings in it. The other three could not be found anywhere, even though she was the only one in the house and remembered distinctly removing the five the night before.

On another morning, Susan was about to take a shower but stopped suddenly when she distinctly heard voices. "Who could that be?" she wondered. Stepping from the bathroom and walking into the adjacent bedroom, she found the radio on. She had not turned it on and it had not been set to come on. Almost without thinking she said aloud: "OK, Joe, you turned the radio on--you can turn the thing off!" She abruptly turned and went back to her shower. When she returned, the radio was off.

On another occasion, she experienced even more playful behavior. She was in the bathroom when suddenly her nightgown, which hung on a hook across the room, flew across the intervening space and landed on her head! Susan was the only one in the room; in fact, she was the only one in the house! Doors and windows were closed, so she knew that a draft of air could not have been the cause.

If strange things had happened only to Susan, she might have passed it off as strictly her imagination. But soon her son, Mark, who sometimes stayed at the house, also began to experience things. One episode that he remembers vividly involved one of the family cats, named Jello.

Jello was one of those furry felines that liked to be let outside and then back in several times during the day. When Joe was still living he complained frequently about always having to let the cats out and then back in. Well, after Joe's passing, his son Mark came downstairs one morning to find Jello waiting impatiently to go out. He let the cat out and went back upstairs, but returned a short time later to let the cat back in. Imagine his surprise when he came down the stairs to find Jello already in, sitting patiently on the mat by the door. Incredibly, this experience happened not just once, but several times, with no explanation.

As time passed, Susan and her son experienced fewer and fewer things out of the ordinary. She remains convinced that her husband had, indeed, come back to haunt the house--at least for a time.

Without warning one of the doors creaked . . .

"MARGARET"

The Old Commercial Building is one of Galena's oldest. Part of the structure is log, now covered with clapboards nearly as old. Nestled against the Galena river bluff, you hardly notice until you're upon it. A family who owned the home in the 1980s thoroughly enjoyed the house, but they traveled a lot, and so it remained vacant much of the time. On occasion, their teenage daughter, Kelly, would be the only one at the house, but strangely, she soon refused to stay there alone.

The family responded by asking a friend, Gloria, to stay with Kelly whenever she was at the house alone. This was fine with Kelly, who quickly settled in with Gloria that first night. Both were in the master bedroom upstairs looking at magazines to get ideas for Kelly's prom dress. They were busily engaged in this endeavor when suddenly the peace and quiet of the home was interrupted by a large crash coming from the downstairs. Gloria was alarmed, fearing that the cat may have tipped over a piece of furniture.

"No," said Kelly, "that's just Margaret, our ghost." She proceeded to explain that sometimes the doorbell would mysteriously ring, the shutters would close and other strange things would happen. A quick check downstairs by Gloria confirmed that nothing was out of order. "Really," laughed Kelly, "these things just happen."

Gloria encountered nothing more out of the ordinary until a few months later. She was again staying at the house and was watching TV in the master bedroom. Nearby, in the same room, was a large wooden wardrobe, or armoire. Without warning, one of the doors creaked! Looking over, Gloria saw that the door was open a couple of inches. This startled her because the doors were heavy and did not swing by themselves.

Her attention, however, had returned to the television when she heard yet another creak. This time the door was open six to eight inches! Gloria lay there staring at the door when it happened again! Remembering her conversations with Kelly, she jumped up, went over to the half-open door, and proclaimed: "Margaret, you're not scaring me away!" Much to her surprise, the door immediately flew entirely open and a blast of cold air rushed past her.

Regaining her composure, Gloria repeated her admonition: "Margaret, you're not scaring me away!" Having said that, she promptly jumped into bed and pulled the covers over her head! Nothing more happened that night.

On one other occasion, another woman, Elma, was staying with Gloria for a short time at the house. This individual seemed uncomfortable with the house, but Gloria didn't realize how much so until she awoke at 4:30 A.M. and Elma was nowhere to be found!

Finally, she was located out on the front walk, shoveling

snow. When asked whatever for, Elma replied: "Well, I'm not going back into that house. You can bring my suitcases down to the car. I'll meet you at Clark's Restaurant at 7 A.M." No amount of prodding could get Elma to elaborate. But Gloria knew. It was Margaret . . .

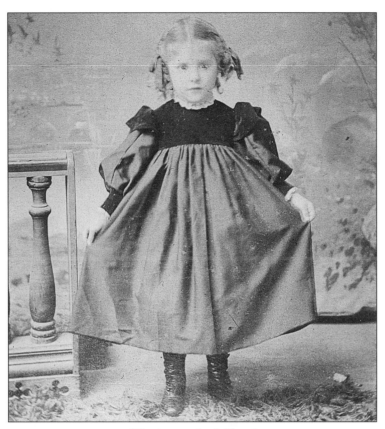

"That's enough, children!"

"CHILDREN AT PLAY"

Barbara has been involved with Galena and its business community for over fourteen years. She had never been a believer in ghosts, but a couple of personal experiences, combined with that of several friends, have caused her to reconsider.

Her experience involved a main street business property. The building in question is typical of those pre-Civil War brick buildings which line Galena's main street. Many owners and many businesses have played a part in its history. Perhaps the only unusual period of occupancy, if you can call it such, was right after the turn-of-the-century when a funeral home took up residence in one portion of the building.

Barbara, along with Kay, her mother, and Ron, a realtor, were looking to invest in such a property. Ron knew the building well, but since he was tied up at the office Barbara went with another realtor for a showing. She viewed the one building, but upon entering the doorway of the adjoining building, abruptly stopped and said, "I don't want this building." The realtor laughed as he walked in behind her, but Barbara turned and left repeating, "I don't want it!" Although she could not explain it, Barbara had sensed something that she did not like.

Both returned to the real estate office where Barbara proceeded to tell Ron that she did not like the feeling of the building and did not want to own it. The two men laughed, especially when they told Barbara that the one adjoining building had been a mortuary. It took Ron, however, six months to convince her to reconsider and invest in the property.

Despite continued reservations, Barbara joined her partners and purchased the building. It wasn't long, however, before others experienced things that could not readily be explained. Barbara's mother, Kay, entered the building to open up early one morning and stopped suddenly. She heard children laughing and playing. She thought this odd, because no one else was supposed to be in the building. A look outside confirmed her distinct impression that the sound was coming from within. It sounded like the children were upstairs.

Kay carefully climbed the stairs to the second floor, but still could not locate the sound. She then climbed to the third floor, but still no children. Returning to the second floor, she suddenly sensed the sound of children giggling. It was really a very pleasant sound, not at all threatening. She stood at the top of the steps and listened for a while and smiled. It sounded as if children were playing on a playground.

Kay then returned to the first floor, stopped, and clapped her hands: "That's enough, children!" she said aloud. The sound of children stopped. Kay heard the sounds of these playful children on two separate occasions.

On another occasion, Barbara received a call from a very nervous employee who asked if she could close the store at 4 P.M.--one hour early. Jane was quite upset and wanted to leave the store right away. Barbara, surprised, asked if she was ill. "No", Jane replied, "I heard them!" Again she repeated: "I heard them!"

To close at the regular time would have meant staying in the building until after dark, and this was something that she did not want to do. Jane described in detail exactly what Barbara's mother had encountered--children's voices, seemingly at play. Surprisingly, Jane was unaware of what any others had heard or experienced.

Barbara herself came to hear voices, too. Upon entering the building one day, she heard two men and a woman talking. At first, she thought they were passing by the back door of the building, for she was the only one in the building. "But, no," she thought, "the sound of their voices is definitely coming from the first floor!" And these were not distant, muffled voices. They were clear and distinct.

Barbara carefully followed the sounds over to the back counter, where they seemed to be originating. Reaching over to the wall, she turned on the light switch, immediately bathing the entire area in light. The voices abruptly stopped. They did not return.

Barbara remembers one other incident in this building. She was up on a ladder to better position a new quilt for display. No one else was on the floor. Suddenly, she sensed someone walk behind her. "Hello," she said, "I'll be down in a minute." Climbing down the ladder, she turned to see who had come in. There was no one. Thinking perhaps it was her imagination, she continued her work, moving the ladder to attend to the other side of the quilt. No sooner had she climbed back up than she experienced the same feeling. "It was as if someone had moved past right behind me," she remembered. But again, there was no one else on the floor. Barbara still has no explanation.

"PAULA"

(When we requested permission to print this fascinating story, Skip and Carol generously consented. In addition, Skip wrote: "We have no problems with your using our names in the piece. After experiencing the slings and arrows of running for national office, we feel that no harm can come to us from the accurate rendition of a true (and still to me-- astonishing) story." Here follows, then, their story:)

Skip and Carol bought their farm, along with the old farm house, in 1968. With the exception of the previous 10 years, the farm had been in one family, the Herman Becker family, for over half a century. Herman and his second wife, Emma, were in the nursing home at Elizabeth at the time. His first wife was Paula Rowe, who had died in the house after several years of marriage.

The house is about 135 years old and was in terribly poor condition when Skip and Carol purchased it. They considered tearing it down, but decided on renovation instead. They worked on it for about three months, doing everything. Wiring, plumbing, heating--all had to be completely replaced.

After about one year, they began to notice lights that would be "on" when they knew they had been turned off. Invariably they would ask the kids: "Hey, who left the lights on?" No one, however, had. One day their daughter, Caren, who was about seven years of age, got up in the morning and asked why her mother had come into the room during the middle of the night to check on her. Carol, however, had been nowhere near the room. In less than a week, their son, Rick, asked the same question one morning about his room. His mother had not been near his room, either.

It wasn't too long after this that they heard footsteps in the attic. Gaining access to the attic at this time meant crawling up through a small door in the ceiling of the room below. There was standing head room under the peak of the

*Suddenly, the streaks of light around the door were broken
by the outline of a human . . .*

roof only; there really wasn't room enough for anyone to walk around up there. There was only one light bulb up there that provided some light for whoever poked their head up through the trap door.

Imagine their further surprise when a neighbor, who frequently drove by on the road out front, asked why their attic light was on. Skip checked and sure enough, it was.

This continued, with the family hearing footsteps about once each month. At the same time, they'd find that attic light on.

Things got serious about 1971-72 when in the middle of the night Skip and Carol both awoke with a start. Skip said: "There's somebody in the room!" Both were sitting bolt upright in bed by this time. They could both feel it. While the door to their bedroom was closed, the hall light was always left on. As a result they could see the cracks of light around three sides of the bedroom door. Suddenly, they saw these streaks of light broken by the outline of a human, just as if a person had walked in front of the door, temporarily blocking the light. Both saw the same thing. Skip immediately turned and hit the light switch. There was absolutely nothing in the room. They were alone. Needless to say, neither got any more sleep that night.

Understandably, this activity got the whole family thinking about ghosts and the past history of the house. Then one day Skip was talking to someone who remembered some of the details of Herman Becker's first wife, Paula. She had died in the house after a short illness. During the wake her body lay where the TV room now was. Not too long afterwards, Herman married Emma.

Family discussions ensued, in which Skip's family agreed that they must have a spirit of some kind. They were also agreed that it was feminine and benign. There was a consensus that it must be Paula. Everyone, however, was sworn to secrecy because of what the neighbors might say and the difficulty of selling a haunted house should that ever be necessary.

It was in 1974, however, that word got out. The family was vacationing on the West Coast and had a friend watching over the place. Jack had helped out before, but never before for any length of time.

While in Oregon, Skip called home to see how everything was going. After some small talk about how fine everything was, Jack abruptly asked: "What the hell is going on in this house? I go to bed and all the lights go on downstairs, even in the basement. I go down, turn them off, and a couple of hours later--they're all on again!"

Skip calmly said, "Don't worry, everything's fine, I'll explain when we get home." Skip did explain and asked Jack not to tell, but somehow, the story got around. In fact, all around. While at the grocery store one day, the check-out clerk calmly said, "Well, I understand you've been getting some visits from Aunt Paula . . ." Skip groaned . . .

Herman Becker and his second wife, Emma, were both very elderly and still in the nursing home at this time, but she shortly died. Almost immediately, Skip and the family noticed that things were quieting down. And then Herman died. And at that point everything stopped. Since that time, they have experienced nothing more. Evidently Paula's spirit was reunited with the others . . . and is now at rest.